ASIAN ANIMALS

TIGERS

Alicia Rodriguez

TABLE OF CONTENTS

Sight Words.......................2
Words to Know.....................3
Index.............................16

A Pelican Book

SEAHORSE PUBLISHING

Teaching Tips for Caregivers and Teachers:

Research shows that one of the best ways for students to learn a new topic is to read about it.

Before Reading

- Read the title and predict what the book will be about.
- Read the "Words to Know" and discuss the meaning of each word.
- Read the back cover to see what the book is about.

During Reading

- When a student gets to a word that is unknown, ask them to look at the rest of the sentence to find clues to help with the meaning of the unknown word.
- Motivate students with praise and encouragement.

After Reading

- Discuss the main idea of the book.
- Ask students to give one detail that they learned in the book.

Sight Words

a	can	long	them
all	have	or	they
also	help	play	this
be	is	run	to
big	jump	some	white
black	like	that	

Words to Know

claws

orange

paws

stripes

tiger

This is a **tiger**.

tiger

Tigers can be **orange** or white.

orange

All tigers have black **stripes**.

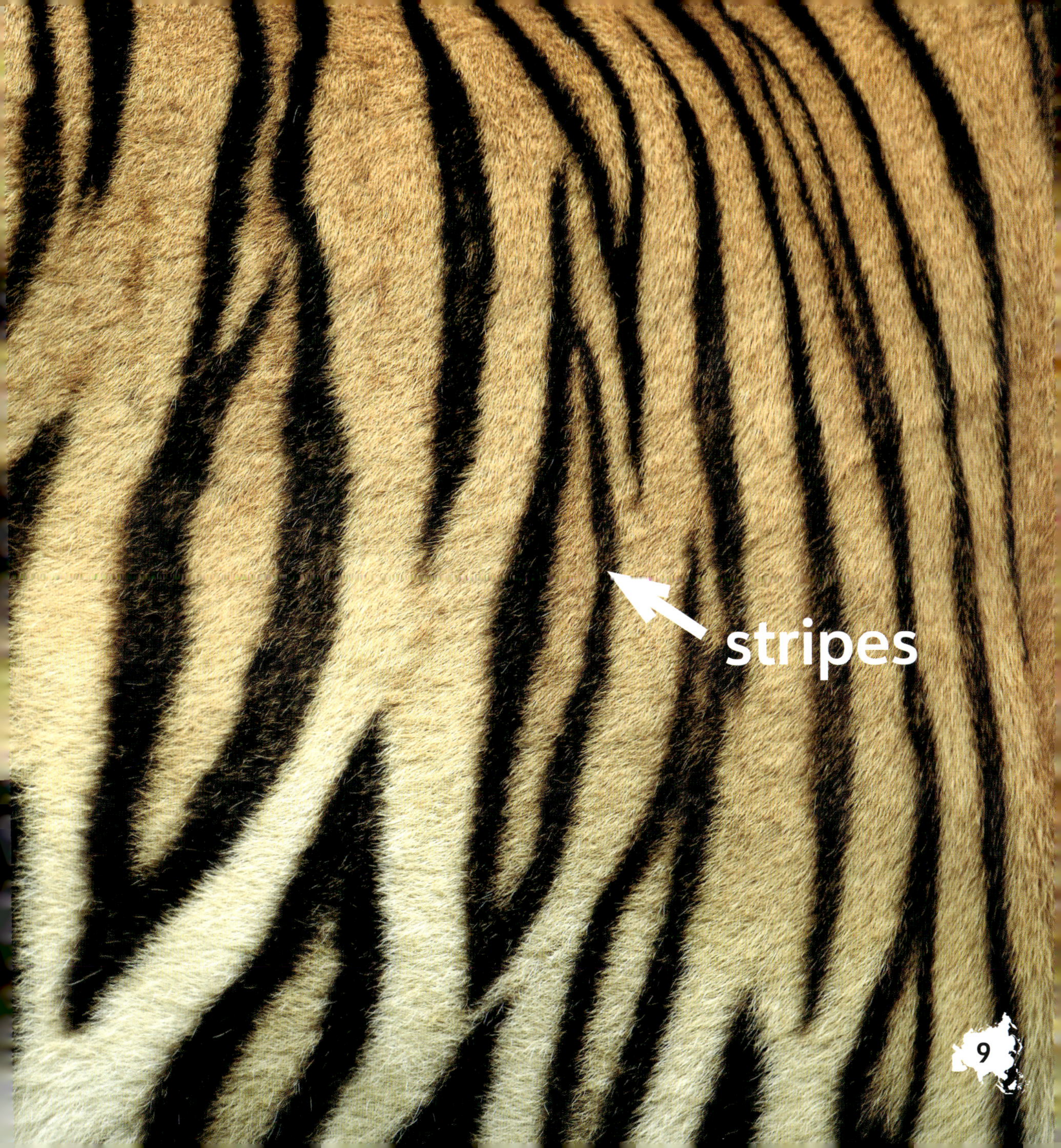
stripes

Tigers have big **paws** that help them run.

paw

They also have big, long **claws**.

claws

Some tigers like to play.

All tigers can jump!

Index

black 8
jump 15
play 14
run 10
tiger(s) 4, 5, 6, 8, 10, 14, 15

Written by: Alicia Rodriguez
Design by: Under the Oaks Media
Series Development: James Earley
Editor: Kim Thompson

Photos: Shutterstock: Terry Granger: cover; Ondrej Prosicky: p. 5; Vasilieva Tatiana: p. 6-7; dangdumrong: p. 9; apple2499: p. 11; Suntisook.D: p. 13; julian W: p. 14; Bernard Richter: p. 15

Library of Congress PCN Data
Tigers / Alicia Rodriguez
Asian Animals
ISBN 978-1-63897-436-9(hard cover)
ISBN 978-1-63897-551-9(paperback)
ISBN 978-1-63897-666-0(EPUB)
ISBN 978-1-63897-781-0(eBook)
Library of Congress Control Number: 2022933727

Printed in the United States of America.

Seahorse Publishing Company
www.seahorsepub.com

Published in the United States
Seahorse Publishing
PO Box 771325
Coral Springs, FL 33077

SEAHORSE PUBLISHING